CW01337232

In the Stillness

poems, prayers,
reflections

Elizabeth Mills

Inner Light Books
San Francisco, California

2018

In the Stillness
poems, prayers, reflections
© 2018 Elizabeth Mills
All Rights Reserved

Except for brief quotations, no part of this publication may be reproduced, stored in a retrieval system, or transmitted, in any form or by any means, electronic, mechanical, photocopy, recorded, or otherwise, without prior written permission.

Editor: Charles Martin
Copy Editor: Kathy McKay
Layout and design: Matt Kelsey

Published by Inner Light Books
San Francisco, California
www.innerlightbooks.com

editor@innerlightbooks.com

ISBN 978-1-7328239-0-7 (hardcover)
ISBN 978-1-7328239-1-4 (paperback)
ISBN 978-1-7328239-2-1 (eBook)

Scripture quotations marked (KJV) are taken from the Authorized (King James) Version. Rights in the Authorized Version in the United Kingdom are vested in the Crown. Reproduced by permission of the Crown's patentee, Cambridge University Press.

Scripture quotations marked (NRSV) are taken from the New Revised Standard Version Bible, copyright © 1989 National Council of the Churches of Christ in the United States of America. Used by permission. All rights reserved worldwide.

Scripture quotations marked (NIV) are taken from the Holy Bible, New International Version®, NIV®. Copyright © 1973, 1978, 1984, 2011 by Biblica, Inc.™ Used by permission of Zondervan. All rights reserved worldwide. www.zondervan.com. The "NIV" and "New International Version" are trademarks registered in the United States Patent and Trademark Office by Biblica, Inc.™

These words have been written in times of quiet prayer, and they are offered with love. I hope that in some way these words may be helpful to you and encourage your own spiritual journey.

EMM 2018

"And the end of words is to bring men to the knowledge of things, beyond what words can utter."

Isaac Penington

Contents

1. In the Stillness

2. This Day and Every Day

3. The Space Within

4. What If . . .

>   Part One
>   Heaven
>   Our Lives in His Life
>   Part Two
>   Earth
>   His Life in Our Lives

5. Gifts

6. Love

In the Stillness

In the stillness
Is the Pearl of Great Price
Where the Light shines . . .
It is within us all
But we must dig deep

It does not lie on the surface
Where it would be trampled over
It is secure within
Protected by our very selves
So often unaware

Yet search and look
And we shall find
This Simple Gift (of Love) within

Give your all
And treasure it with all you have to give
Love it, tend it, care for it
That it may grow and shine
This tender seed, this Precious Gift
This treasure trove of Love
Found simply alive
Within . . .

For where your treasure is, there your heart will be also.
Matthew 6:21 (NIV)

This Day and Every Day

"There are more things in heaven and earth, Horatio, than are dreamt of in your philosophies."

William Shakespeare

Come
Be still

And know
That I am God

Be quiet and attune your heart
To the Spirit
Who waits for you
And greets you with Love

This day and every day
Amen

Looking for God means living
With a different perspective
Seeing from a new viewpoint
One that always looks to the horizon
And sees beyond . . .

Be far-sighted
But allow the Eyes of Heaven
To direct your gaze
And bring new vision and clear sight

This day and every day
Amen

Keep the flame of Prayer
Burning in your heart
And the flame of His Love alive in you
So that your heart may be on fire
With the Love of God

This day and every day
Amen

Dear Lord
Help me to be quiet and still
And to wait on You . . .

To listen for Your Voice, calling
In the wilderness of life

May Your Spirit be both My Rock
And My Shield

That I may walk in your Light
And live in Your Truth

This day and every day
Amen

The Real Life
The Life that is beyond,
Beneath, above and around
Will sustain and hold us always

This day and every day
Amen

Make time to be still
And to abide within
With the Spirit of Truth
Which is Love

This day and every day
Amen

Dip into the River of Silence
Be cleansed, refreshed, renewed

This day and every day
Amen

Breathe deeply of the Spirit
For it can fill you with its Life
Allow it to permeate your mind
And your heart
And bring you Peace
See it flowing through your body
Filling every cell with its Love

This day and every day
Amen

May your heart be pure
Your life simple
And your mind grateful
Seek to keep Me
At the centre of every part of your life
And listen for My Word
Ever spoken gently in the hearts
Of those who will listen
Keep Me in your heart and your mind
And in your life always

This day and every day
Amen

The Kingdom of Heaven is within you
His Spirit is within you
His Life with yours
See how the two intertwine
When you dedicate yourself to Him
His Life will live within you

This day and every day
Amen

May I take time to be quiet
That I may hear
Your Spirit whispering

That I may know clearly
Your Wisdom and Your Joy

That this day may be Yours
And every day that follows too . . .
Amen

If you come to Him
In the silence of your heart
There you will find His Spirit
Waiting
In quietness
For your spirit is in His Heart
And His Spirit is in your heart

This day and every day
Amen

Keep your eyes fixed on Him
At all times
He is pure Goodness
Allow His Power to strengthen you
And His Love to guide you

This day and every day
Amen

Lord, please help me to be the best I can be
Not through striving or reaching
So much as gently and simply waiting
On Your Words of Wisdom
And then just trying to let them
Be alive in me

This day and every day
Amen

Where does your treasure lie?
In gold and riches?
In prestige and fame?
Is your treasure in outward things
Or does your treasure lie within?

Do you recognise the wealth inside
That which is to be honoured within
Is it worth giving all that you have?
Is it worth listening?
Is it worth attending to?

It is worth everything
Its value priceless
It is of the kind that will not decay or die
It is what will always be there
Not visible — but eternal —
And of eternal value

This day and every day
Amen

*G*o deep into the silence
The silence that heals
The silence that listens
The silence that Loves

All that is found in the silence is unconditional
All that is offered in the silence is free

It is the Great gift
There — for the taking

Only we must avail ourselves of it
And become still

In the silence of the heart
God speaks

And so it is
And always shall be

This day and every day
Amen

It is not mediated by man
It is given by God

It is in all
And yet beyond all

It is simple
Yet profound

It is Real
And Alive
Vibrant and true

But
It is hidden and must be sought

And when found, must, above all else,
Be treasured

It is the Greatest Gift

This day and every day
Amen

Listen every day
To the Voice that echoes within you
Hear Wisdom,
Peace,
Truth
And Love
Allow it to be
Your Guiding Light

This day and every day
Amen

Come, He says, and rest . . .

Enter into the Silence
Where He waits
Join your heart with His
And Be Still
And Know

Know that He is God
And that He waits
In simplicity
For us to come

And when we do
He welcomes us
Welcomes us Home

Home to Him
Home in Him
Home with Him

This day and every day
Amen

Dance with the Divine Spirit
Every day

Let Her Light shine
And Her Joy radiate
Through all your pain
And sorrows

And may She feed
Your innermost being

This day and every day
Amen

Deep within is a tiny seed
In darkness
Not seen

It is Treasure within

For this small seed
Has Abundant Life
And feeds us from within

Small though it may seem
This germ of Life
Is ready to burst forth

And bring us
Beauty, Joy and Peace

This day and every day
Amen

Let stillness always be in your heart
This stilling of the outer
To taste the Joy within

For this Joy is constant
And the life within ever present
Amidst the changing scenes without

Seek the Joy of Stillness
And the deeper life to which it leads

This day and every day
Amen

Come to the table of the Lord
Where good things are laid out
And we can feast
But so often we keep away
Won't go near
For fear of ridicule
Or lack of faith

Walk slowly towards . . .
One step at a time
But keep moving
In the direction
In which we are beckoned
And know that all is offered freely
And it is given with Love

This day and every day
Amen

What are you afraid of?
Where does the fear come from?

The world of mirrors
Flashes and shines
But is illusion
Not real
And will pass
See beyond the reflections
To the core
The single pure Reality
From which all else stems
And to which all else returns

Above all else and
Through all else
Trust in this Reality
Which manifests an
Inner Light and Radiance
Which may be apprehended In Love
And known through Silence

This day and every day
Amen

Know that as you breathe
So God Breathes too . . .

And each outward breath of the Spirit
May be an inward breath for you

A sign to you of His Presence
An awareness of His Life in yours

This day and every day
Amen

Abide in the quiet place of your heart
Where the Spirit dwells
And waits quietly
To be found

This is no game
Where the Spirit hides while you seek

When you look, you will find
When you knock,
The door will open to you

This day and every day
Amen

There is the faith that believes
God is outside ourselves
Perhaps even a distant figure
One we can never reach

And there is the understanding
That we are part of God
And God is part of us

This day and every day
Amen

Sit at His Feet
Learn from Him

For His Yoke is easy
He is gentle and humble of heart

Bring all your anxieties to Him
Lay them at His Feet
And let them go

Know that all things are safe
In His Keeping

Trust Him with your life
Your Very Life

This day and every day
Amen

Let all things begin in Silence
Raising one's heart and mind
To the Greater Reality
To the Love of God
In our midst

This day and every day
Amen

Let me be alone with this candle
That represents Your Love
Like two in love
Who want only to be together
To see each other
And spend time in one another's company

So, Lord, let me be like this with You
That You are my heart's desire
And I recognize my need of You
Above all else

This day and every day
Amen

Be refreshed and renewed
Through stillness . . .

Be strengthened and sustained
Through stillness . . .

Be energized and embraced
Through silence . . .

Be calmed and cherished
Through silence . . .

Bring Stillness and Silence
To the centre of your life

This day and every day
Amen

Make yourself smaller
The less there is of you
The more room there is for Him . . .

This day and every day
Amen

Who are You dear Lord
But Love
What do You bring dear Lord
But Love
What do You teach dear Lord
But Love

How do we approach you dear Lord
But through Love
How do we seek You dear Lord
But through Love
How do we follow You dear Lord
But through Love

Love You give
And Love You show
And we must do the same
If we are to follow You

There is no other way of knowing You
But to love You
There is no way to follow You
But through loving others

This day and every day
Amen

See this beautiful Love
Like a circle
Constantly moving
Evolving
Intertwining
And then returning to its original form
After all that has happened
It is unchanged
For it is constant
Steady and true
Always available
And Ever Present

This day and every day
Amen

Nothing can change its Essence
Or its heart
It can give itself away
Yet remain complete
Such is Love
Infinite Love
Given once
Yet always offered
Unchanging
And True

This day and every day
Amen

You are a Song of Love
Sung constantly

We only have to listen

And we may begin to hear
Your Melody

And then begin to dance
To Your Tune

This day and every day
Amen

Pure clear water
Entering our hearts
Such is the Love of the Spirit
Finding its Way
Through the cracks
And crevices of our lives

This day and every day
Amen

Love will find us
But we must want to be found

There may be a desire in our hearts to look
This is the signal that we want to be found
That we are holding up our hands
And calling out
So then, Love will come
And rescue us
Pick us up
And hold us
Restore our inward being
And help us to walk again
Guide us to a place where we can know
Always
The comfort and Love of the Spirit
And its Guiding Hand in our lives

This day and every day
Amen

Breathe deeply of the Spirit
It is Love

Breathe deeply of the Spirit
It is Joy

Breathe deeply of the Spirit
It is Healing

Breathe deeply

Make space in your life for the Spirit
It is Peace

Make space in your life for the Spirit
It brings Grace

Make space

Find stillness in each day
It brings Life

Find stillness

This day and every day
Amen

Love whispers
Quietly
For all to hear

Each and every person
Can attune their hearts
And listen

But this takes time
And dedication
And a strong desire

Like waiting
Listening for the birdsong
Which can resonate

Touch our hearts
And stir us
To want more

Listen!
For the Spirit is singing
In whispers of Love

This day and every day
Amen

There is a joy in silence
When there appears to be nothing going on
From the outside

Inside there is a party
A celebration
A reunion

There are no words to describe this joy
It can only be known
Experienced

It may not come easily
But persevere
For the Joy is there

And waits to welcome us into
The Warmth of its Embrace

Come and feel
The immediacy of this Love
And the effervescence of the Spirit

Overflowing with sparkle
And delight
At the intimacy of meeting
And the presence of Love within

This day and every day
Amen

If I were to sit and wait
Would You come?

Would I see Your Face again?
The Face I love the most
The Face that shines like no other

There is a kindness in Your Eyes
There is a warmth that radiates out

Of course, I do not know
But this is how it feels
This is how it always seems

You are not visible
But that does not mean You are not present

The warmth shines through in feeling
And the light radiates out in love

It is not a case of will You come
What matters is that I come
And that I sit and wait.

This day and every day
Amen

I feel as if I know You
And yet I cannot

Yet what You have shown me
Is all that I need
It may only be a small part
Infinitesimal
But it fills me

It brings hope to my mind
And love to my heart
For there is so much given in even an inkling
A glimmer shines forever

Small does not mean insignificant
For the measure that You bring
Is always enough

A drop in Your Ocean of Love
Is a continuous flow of supply for us

Like the loaves and the fishes
There is always Abundance
From which we receive
And in which we are fed and nurtured

This day and every day
Amen

The Spirit of God is ever present
But are we?

How do we seek Him?
With our hearts open
Or with our minds closed

Expecting a Response
Or doubting it possible

Waiting on Him
But looking elsewhere

Talking of Him
But not listening for Him

Lord, help to mend my brokenness
Put me together Lord
In You

So that I may seek you with my whole heart
And listen for Your Voice
Ever present in my life

This day and every day
Amen

Dear Lord
Help me to be Your servant always
Not thinking of myself
So much as listening for Your Will
Not looking at my own needs
So much as thinking of the needs of others

Help me Lord to live and move
According to Your Direction
According to Your Leadings
For You are my Father
And You are my Guide

Without you I am lost
Without You I am nothing
With You I am made whole and
With You I can see more clearly

This day and every day
Amen

Help me Lord
Not to focus on my darkness
But on Your Light
Nor on my frailty
But on Your Strength
Let me always look to You
For all that I need

This day and every day
Amen

You give to me
I receive
I give to others
You receive

Here is the Constant Flow of Love
Created by You
Given by You
And returned to You

Help me, above all,
To love You
And so to love others
In the Power of Your Love

This day and every day
Amen

On our own
We can do so little
Or so it seems

Yet each small action
Makes a difference
Each small action
Adds up
No longer small
But magnified

The small action of one
Is like a small light
Shining
In the darkness of the world

But as each light spreads
So Goodness grows
And darkness is diminished

This day and every day
Amen

Whom do you seek?
I seek the Risen Christ . . .
He is not here . . .
He is everywhere
In all places
At all times
Never limit Him in your thinking
Know that wherever you are
He is with you
In every circumstance of your life
He is with you
Seek always to be His Servant
Living in His Love
And in His Truth

This day and every day
Amen

As you seek My Spirit
So I am here

As you seek My Love
So it is with you

As you seek My Heart
So it is open to yours

As you seek My Way
So I will make it known to you

As you seek Me
So you will know the Truth
Of all that I bring

This day and every day
Amen

Lord, I know that I need You
But sometimes I forget
And go my own way
But when I get lost
I need You more
And need Your Love again

Teach me to live in such a way
That I never forget my need of You
Not only when I remember
But in my life always

May I be truly grateful
For the Love You bring
Alongside me on my journey

This day and every day
Amen

Listen to the Silence . . .
 . . . It will teach you

Listen to the Silence . . .
 . . . Here wounds are gently healed

Listen to the Silence . . .
 . . . It will bring your life alive

Listen to the Silence . . .
 . . . And know the Peace it brings

Listen to the Silence . . .
 . . . You will find Love

This day and every day
Amen

Dear Lord
In the midst of my struggles
I come to You
In the midst of my pain
I come to You.
In the midst of my anxiety
I come to You

There are many things that are so hard

Help me Lord to turn to You
To remember that You are always present
That Your Love will never leave me
And You will bring me
All that I need

I ask for Your Strength
I ask for Your Peace
And most of all
I ask for Your Love

Fill me dear Lord
With Your Presence

Help me to know You are holding my hand
And stay with me
All the days of my life

Amen

The Space Within

What may appear to be empty
Is more than enough
For a lifetime

What may appear to be nothing
Is all we shall ever need

The space within is like a desert
Waiting for water

The space within is like a mountain
Waiting to be climbed

The space within is precious
And waits only to be discovered

And then explored
For the duration of the journey
We call life

The kingdom of God is within you.
Luke 17:21 (KJV)

What If . . .

PART ONE

HEAVEN

Our Lives in His Life

"Joy of Heaven to Earth come down."
Charles Wesley

WHAT IF . . .

Jesus was not the Son of God
But a son of God,

Loved, nurtured, cherished and guided

In the same way that we are sons
And daughters of God

Open to the Spirit of God
As He always was
And perhaps that is the difference

That He was always open
Whereas we are constantly clouded
And busy with the world

Seek first his kingdom.
Matthew 6:33 (NIV)

WHAT IF . . .

His Words symbolize Truth
    He is Bread . . .
        and feeds us
    He is Light . . .
        and illumines our path
    He is the Good Shepherd . . .
        who cares for us
    He is the Gate . . .
        and opens up a way for us

And what if the reality of these words is far simpler than we think . . .

In the beginning was the Word.
John 1:1 (KJV)

WHAT IF . . .

I and the Father are One

    Opens up a way of living for us too . . .

Where we are,
    through prayer and openness,
    through seeking first the Kingdom of God,

Creates a way through which God can
    Work in us . . .

    For His Glory always
      Of course

Apart from me you can do nothing.
John 15:5 (NIV)

WHAT IF . . .

He was not God and Man

    He was a man,
             but a man
        Totally overshadowed and inspired by
            the Spirit of God

And what if the possibility of being human
      But also open to God's inspiration and
Presence
           is available to us all . . .
           NOW

   If we seek Him in the silence of our hearts . . .

       Be still, and know that I am God.
            Psalm 46:10 (KJV)

WHAT IF . . .

What matters most about His Ministry
    Is not what He said
        But how He lived

Times of quiet . . .
        regularly punctuated by times with others

Times of silence . . .
        interspersed with words spoken

Times seeking the Unseen
        Leading to visible interactions

Times of attunement with His Father
        Inspiring insights to be shared . . .

        I am the way, the truth, and the life.
        John 14:6 (KJV)

WHAT IF...

His Death leads the Way for ours?

That not only He passed from death to life
        But that this aspect of His Life
                Also points the way for ours...

That we too *rise* from the *dead*
        That we do not *sleep* in Him
                Rather we live in Him

In the twinkling of an eye
        We too are re-born
                And New Life awaits...

Behold, I make all things new.
Revelation 21:5 (KJV)

WHAT IF . . .

Healings and miracles are not extraordinary
    Not only a product of this Man

What if they are rather
    A natural outpouring
        Of a life lived in the Spirit

Where one seeks a greater good
    Where one seeks the Intervention of the Higher
        Into the every day

Where all things are possible
    Where every bush is aglow
        with the Glory of God

With God all things are possible.
Matthew 19:26 (KJV)

WHAT IF . . .

We limit our thinking
      By thinking of Him only in history
            As a man who lived 2,000 years
   ago

What if we do better to see Him as Now
      Present in our lives
            Administering His Love to us

Welcoming all people NOW
      Forgiving us all in each moment

What if He is 'Now'
      Rather than 'then'

          I am with you always.
              Matthew 28:20 (KJV)

WHAT IF . . .

He seeks to turn our lives upside down?

    To turn our water into wine
        To walk with us each day

    To call us to follow Him now
        To minister to our needs . . .

Come with me by yourselves to a quiet place.
Mark 6:31 (NIV)

His Way is

Simple
Direct
Loving
Challenging
Enriching
Enfolding
Clear

And He calls us to it

Now
Every day
In each moment
Always
Constantly
Forever

Amen

PART TWO

EARTH

His Life in Our Lives

"Breathe on me, Breath of God."
Edwin Hatch

WHAT IF . . .

We knew that there is a spiritual world
Interacting with our own . . .

What difference would it make . . .
To how we act, to how we think
And how we live our daily lives

So we look not only at what is all around
But seek also what is not visible
And yet is present
In each moment
That we live in this physical world

And is waiting for us
When we leave

In him we live and move and have our being
Acts 17:28 (NRSV)

WHAT IF . . .

We really listened
To the echoes of the silent land
Deep within us

And allowed this to be
Our Guiding Light

And to know it to be
The Haven
Within our very own hearts

A place of safety
Love and Peace

Heaven in our midst

Hear, and your soul shall live.
Isaiah 55:3 (KJV)

WHAT IF . . .

We learned to love first
Above and beyond all else

So that we see the good
In one another
Rather than the faults

And we learned to live in such a way
That we place others first
Thinking not only of ourselves

But genuinely to care for
The well-being of others

Love thy neighbour as thyself.
Mark 12:31 (KJV)

WHAT IF...

We took things more slowly
Did not rush so much
Gave more time to be

For in our busyness
And in our doing
We miss time to reflect
Time to notice

Time to live

And if we go so fast
We will miss the beauty
And the Treasures along the way

There is a time for everything.
Ecclesiastes 3:1 (NIV)

WHAT IF...

We could learn to forgive
When we have been hurt
And when damage has been done to our hearts
And to our lives

If we could only see
Why others do the harm they do

Realising we are all in some way victims
All frail
All wounded

And all in need of forgiveness

Forgive us our debts, as we forgive our debtors.
Matthew 6:12 (KJV)

WHAT IF . . .

We knew how much help there was available
From the Unseen Realms

Would we turn in this direction more
often?
Seek not so much to act in our own
strength
As to understand our need for support

Given in any direction
And for any part of our lives

For it is when we realise our own
weakness
That we may be filled
With the Strength and Abundance
Of Divine Love

My strength is made perfect in weakness.
2 Corinthians 12:9 (KJV)

WHAT IF . . .

We are each like a candle
And can choose to be lit
And so to shine

Becoming then
A source of light in the world

However small the light may be
The more there are
The more Light spreads

And illumines the darkness

Live as children of light.
Ephesians 5:8 (NRSV)

WHAT IF . . .

We need to be open
For the Divine
To enter in

Not too full of self
That there is no room

Making space
By being humble
And seeking to live
In Simplicity

Asking for Love to flow in
And make its Home
In the centre of our hearts

We will come to them
and make our home with them.
John 14:23 (NRSV)

WHAT IF . . .

We need to change our approach to God
Our way of thinking about *Him*

Freeing our minds of preconceptions

Not seeing a gap, distance and remoteness
But feeling a closeness, an intimacy and a warmth

This *God* then,
No longer in a box of our making
Is now *freed*
To be known as our Companion,
Our Friend and our Love

I have called you friends.
John 15:15 (KJV)

WHAT IF . . .

When we pray
We listen more
And speak less

Demand less of God
And open ourselves to receive from God
And learn His Ways

If we are to be attentive to God
We must place ourselves in His Love
And be receptive to His Voice

My sheep listen to my voice.
John 10:27 (NIV)

Our Approach is

In Him
Listening
Loving
Slowly
Forgiving
Asking
Sharing light
Humble
Open-minded
Receptive

And He understands our every step
And welcomes us always

And Finally . . .

WHAT IF . . .

DIVINE INTERVENTION IS MORE COMMON THAN WE THINK!

I will tell of the kindnesses of the LORD.
Isaiah 63:7 (NIV)

The one who calls you is faithful.
1 Thessalonians 5:24 (NRSV)

Gifts

"All good gifts around us are
sent from heaven above."
Matthias Claudius
(translator: Jane M. Campbell)

Gifts

Riches
Riches in Abundance

The Gifts that are given
The Riches poured out

Always with us
Enabling, encouraging

Not transitory
But lasting

Not of greed
But of giving

Not of advantage
But of service

These are the Riches
This is true wealth

Every good and perfect gift is from above.
James 1:17 (NIV)

Beauty

We do not walk alone
For a moment
We walk accompanied
All the time
But so often we do not know
So often we look
But do not see
The Reality in our midst

In the air we breathe
In the life we lead
We are in It
Enfolded
Embraced

He shall give you another Comforter, that he may abide with you for ever.
John 14:16 (KJV)

Real Life!

Life
Real life!
So much is an illusion
All will pass away
But this is real
This will not go
This will remain
This is forever
The Eternal in the midst of life
Every day
If we ask
If we give it room
If we want it with all our hearts
If we seek it above all else
Then it will come and be alive in our life

I have come that they may have life, and have it to the full.
John 10:10 (NIV)

Within

This still point is within for all time
This still point is within for all
This still point is within
This still point is
This still point
This still
This

What is unseen is eternal.
2 Corinthians 4:18 (NIV)

In Quietness and Trust

There is a place of silence
Deep within us all
Where we can go
And listen
To the Word that ever speaks
To the Word that is
Beyond space and time
And yet
Always with us

In quietness and trust is your strength.
Isaiah 30:15 (NIV)

Conversation

In the stillness of our hearts
The Spirit waits

In the stillness of our hearts
The Spirit speaks

In the stillness of our hearts
The Spirit listens

In the stillness of our hearts
There is conversation

*You know him, for he lives with you
and will be in you.*
John 14:17 (NIV)

Simplicity

The Holy Spirit calls us to be simple
To approach God in a simple way
Not to complicate the things of God
But be as little children
Dance for joy
At the blessings that surround us
Trust always in the Love
Which carries us when we are weary
And rejoices with us when we are glad

Unless you change and become like children, you will never enter the kingdom of heaven.
Matthew 18:3 (NRSV)

Nurture

God plants a seed
Within us
Lying unseen
But then there comes a glimmer
Something to encourage it to grow
To break through
And rise above
To see something greater
Something more
Something beyond

The kingdom of heaven is like a mustard seed.
Matthew 13:31 (NRSV)

Prayer

Take time to pray
For this opens the door
Through which many blessings may flow
The Stillness of Prayer is ever present
Underlying all things
But is most deeply near
When we lay aside the matters of the day

When we are busy
It may not be so easy
To keep our door open
But leave it ajar
Or open a window

Keep some form of entry
So we remain open
And receptive
To the Love which flows through
And may enter in
At any time

Pray to your Father, who is unseen.
Matthew 6:6 (NIV)

Pilot Light

There's a tiny light inside
Only a flicker
Easily it can fade
And be extinguished

Yet we may fan it
Keep it alive
If we choose
To take time
And attend

Nurture it
And it will bring warmth
And a glow
Not only to our hearts
But also to the lives of others

Let your light shine.
Matthew 5:16 (NIV)

The Christ Child

He comes to simple places
To be born
He seeks the lowly heart
To make His home

We need to make space in us
For His Spirit to be born
To grow in our hearts
And live among us

Not as a child
But as our Lord
Not as a pauper
But as a King
Ruler of His Kingdom
Where Love is the key
That opens the door
And welcomes us in

Walk humbly with your God.
Micah 6:8 (NRSV)

The Still Small Voice

There is a Voice
Which echoes
Inside every human heart

It is very quiet
And does not speak loudly
But it speaks clearly

We can hear it
If we listen
But we must be very quiet

And we must want to hear it
Seek it out
Make a way clear

It will take time
And dedication
But persevere

For this is worth
All we can give
In each moment

It is the treasure
Of the Voice within
The Still Small Voice
Of God

The LORD was not in the fire: and after the fire a still small voice.
1 Kings 19:12 (KJV)

Love

In all things and at all times
Allow Love in to the centre of your being
So that Love may do its work
From the inside out

"Love was His meaning."
Mother Julian of Norwich

The following poems have been previously published, as indicated.

"In the Stillness"
Quaker Voices 7, no. 3 (May 2016) and
Towards Wholeness 147 (Spring 2017)

"Come Be Still"
The Julian Meetings (December 2015)

"Dear Lord, help me to be quiet and still"
The Julian Meetings (December 2015)

"May I take time"
The Julian Meetings (April 2017)

"Keep your eyes fixed on Him"
Bournemouth Coastal Area Quaker Meeting News and Views (Summer 2015)
Newsletter of the Holy Family Parish, Bournemouth, England (June 2016)
Website of the Holy Family Parish, Bournemouth, England (Lent 2017)

"Go deep into the silence"
Bournemouth Coastal Area Quaker Meeting News and Views (Summer 2017)

"Let stillness"
Quaker Voices 8, no. 2 (March 2017)

"The Space Within"
Quaker Voices 7, no. 2 (March 2016)

"Gifts"
Magazine of St. Mark's Church, Bournemouth, England (March/April 2017)

"Love"
Fellowship of Solitaries Letter 80 (Advent 2016)
Quaker Voices 8, no. 1 (November 2016)

"On our own"
In Stephen Feltham and Peter Wilson, *Moving towards Wholeness* (Friends Fellowship of Healing, 2018)

Elizabeth Mills is a qualified teacher specialising in early childhood education and working with children with special educational needs. She has been a caregiver for many years and currently works as a volunteer for the chaplaincy team in her local hospital. Elizabeth is an ecumenical Christian, and a member of the Religious Society of Friends, and she is actively involved in her local meeting for worship for healing. Her love of stillness has led her to share times of stillness with others through quiet days, Taizé worship, and guided meditations. Writing has always been part of Elizabeth's spiritual journey as she seeks to walk a contemplative path in the midst of daily life. Her poems, prayers, and reflections have appeared in a number of periodicals, magazines, and church newsletters. Elizabeth is married with two children and lives with her husband in Dorset, England.

Also available from Inner Light Books

Walk Humbly, Serve Boldly
Modern Quakers as Everyday Prophets
by Margery Post Abbott
    ISBN 978-0-9998332-6-1, (hardcover) $45
    ISBN 978-0-9998332-7-8, (paperback) $30
    ISBN 978-0-9998332-8-5, (eBook) $12.50

Primitive Quakerism Revived
by Paul Buckley
    ISBN 978-0-9998332-2-3 (hardcover) $25
    ISBN 978-0-9998332-3-0 (paperback)$15
    ISBN 978-0-9998332-5-4 (eBook)$10

Primitive Christianity Revived
by William Penn
Translated into Modern English by Paul Buckley
    ISBN 978-0-9998332-0-9 (hardcover) $25
    ISBN 978-0-9998332-1-6 (paperback) $15
    ISBN 978-0-9998332-4-7 (eBook)$10

Jesus, Christ and Servant of God
Meditations on the Gospel According to John
by David Johnson
    ISBN 978–0–9970604–6–1 (hardcover) $35
    ISBN 978–0–9970604–7–8 (paperback) $25
    ISBN 978–0–9970604–8–5 (eBook) $12.50

The Anti-War
by Douglas Gwyn
    ISBN 978-0-9970604-3-0, (hardcover)$30
    ISBN 978-0-9970604-4-7, (paperback)$17.50
    ISBN 978-0-9970604-5-4, (eBook) $10

Our Life Is Love, the Quaker Spiritual Journey
by Marcelle Martin
    ISBN 978-0-9970604-0-9, (hardcover)$30
    ISBN 978-0-9970604-1-6, (paperback)$17.50
    ISBN 978-0-9970604-2-5, (eBook) $10

A Quaker Prayer Life
by David Johnson
    ISBN 978-0-9834980-5-6 (hardcover) $20
    ISBN 978-0-9834980-6-3 (paperback) $12.50
    ISBN 978-0-9834980-7-0 (eBook)) $10

The Essential Elias Hicks
by Paul Buckley
> ISBN 978-0-9834980-8-7 (hardcover) $25
> ISBN 978-0-9834980-9-4 (paperback) $15
> ISBN 978-0-9970604-9-2 (eBook) $10

The Journal of Elias Hicks
edited by Paul Buckley
> ISBN 978-0-9797110-4-6, (hardcover) $50
> ISBN 978-0-9797110-5-3, (paperback) $30

Dear Friend: The Letters and Essays of Elias Hicks
edited by Paul Buckley
> ISBN 978-0-9834980-0-1 (hardcover) $45
> ISBN 978-0-9834980-1-8 (paperback) $25

The Early Quakers and 'the Kingdom of God'
by Gerard Guiton
> ISBN 978-0-9834980-2-5, (hardcover) $45
> ISBN 978-0-9834980-3-2, (paperback) $25
> ISBN 978-0-9834980-4-9, (eBook) $12.50

John Woolman and the Affairs of Truth
edited by James Proud
> ISBN 978-0-9797110-6-0, (hardcover) $45
> ISBN 978-0-9797110-7-7, (paperback) $25

Cousin Ann's Stories for Children by Ann Preston
edited by Richard Beards
illustrated by Stevie French
> ISBN 978-0-9797110-8-4, (hardcover) $20,
> ISBN 978-0-9797110-9-1, (paperback) $12

Counsel to the Christian-Traveller: also Meditations and Experiences
by William Shewen
> ISBN 978-0-9797110-0-8 (hardcover) $25
> ISBN 978-0-9797110-1-5 (paperback) $15